WHERE AM I GOING?

by Daisy Fields

Copyright © 2018 by Daisy Fields

All rights reserved

ISBN 978-1-62806-177-2

Library of Congress Control Number
2018948579

Salt Water Media
29 Broad Street, Suite 104
Berlin, MD 21811
www.saltwatermedia.com

Cover image by Nick Baker used via
courtesy of www.unsplash.com

Interior photographs by the author and
illustration of the daisy by Jim Adcock

DEDICATION

*Thank you to all the friends and family
who support and challenge me.
You know who you are.*

The things that we do
The things we see
All affect
What we will be
The people we meet
What we see on TV
The places we travel
And what we believe
Who we want to be with
Or maybe alone
Starting a family
Having a home
Trying so hard
To meet our goals
Running so fast
Side stepping black holes

*Isn't it strange, the way people flow
In and out of your life
They come then they go
On what can you depend?
When all things must end
So try to see the good inside
The things that cross
Your path and mind*

We pass through time
Each day we change
We love one another
But then place blame
On the one we think
Has somehow caused all this pain
That really has come
From the hard lives we've been dealt
We have to appreciate
The things we have felt
Things so extreme
It's hard to describe
These feelings I can't believe
Have come from inside
This heart of mine
So full of thoughts
I wonder why they're here
And how long I will have fought

I'm trapped in this place
But dreaming for miles
Keeping my eyes closed
all of the while
the sun is glowing
the sky brilliant with color
a breeze lightly blowing
surrounded by flowers
I lay on the grass
And smell the outside
I hear you behind me
I turn and you hide
You come and join me
In this dream of mine
Where there only is beauty
No such thing as time

*I see you as a glowing beam of light
brightening up my dark room
warm and constant like the sun
as mystic as the moon
I see us walking, down a winding road
toward a world with no end
passing through eternity
and coming 'round again*

with dirty hands
and dirty knees
fading eyes
my heart bleeds
distant future
darkened past
nothing good
ever lasts
past mistakes
flashing bright
who's to know
what is right?
living for me
and no one else
at least I'm free
not just showing what sells
my spirit is mine
and that you can't take
proud of myself
accepting my fate

Life is what we see
somehow wanting more
forever chasing keys
please unlock the door
I'm trapped in here
open your eyes
acknowledge reality
stop the lies
This is what we have
to work with day by day
trying to build permanence
when everyone goes away

The things in this life
keep turning me 'round
looking for truth
lost and found
one solitary flower
on a mountain of stone
trying so hard to grow
feeling alone
lasting through the rain
rising to the light
time passes on
such is this life

Falling through the sky
are golden drops of light
I'm soaring like a bird
in mid-flight
richer than the richest man
surrounded by his things
true happiness
Is something only nature can bring
inspiring is the rain
that cleanses my soul
the future's in the clouds
whisked out of control
blown by the wind
in a cobalt sky
thunder jolts my world
knowing that I.....

*I see you in my darkest hour
you're following me through time
you are to me, a fresh spring day
so infinite, divine
And here I am so lost in life
I don't know what you'll find
for in my heart's a melody
and in my eyes a rhyme
written by god and no one else
I wonder who will know
they'll solve this riddle
with the greatest of ease
and in my heart I'll know
I know that he is here
walking with the wind
and time after time
I'll learn to love again*

And so she kept running
to places unknown
always hiding
the side unshown
past the judges
past the race
past this cold
unloving place
And so she kept running
towards the blue skies
her face to the sun
wide open eyes
to open arms
unconditional love
losing the anger
transcending above

*I look upon the world
and thank it for its change
for the beauty of each season
for all that god has made
time keeps people moving
it will not stop for me
and so I will go forward
keep following the breeze*

so full of life
she flies so high
softest wings
just gliding by
her prayer she sings
a beautiful sound
safe she floats
can't touch the ground

climbing up the mountain
all its twists and turns
this journey is never ending
so many things to learn
through snow and rain
love and blame
time keeps moving on
no second chance to turn around
the past is truly gone

Spinning in circles
the world swallows me
sucked into a black hole
life's a memory
desperately I grip
this one simple strand
tightly I squeeze
it cuts into my hand
I will not let go
it will someday set me free
the string is the light
sent from god to me.

*For all these things
we live and breathe
For all these things
we stay or leave
For all these things
that run our life
For all these things
there is a price
For all these things
as time slips by
For all these things
we laugh and cry
For all these things
a clean slate to start
For all these things
only love in my heart
For all these things
we strive day by day
For all these things
don't get far anyway
For all these things
that one special minute
For all these things
when it comes you're not in it
For all these things
life still goes on
For all these things
morn, after mourn*

For all these things
that come and then go
For all these things
I'm not ready! NO
For all these things
I try to hold on
For all these things
there and then gone
For all these things
I still believe
For all these things
I will achieve.
For all these things
I think and feel
For all these things
that seem so real
For all these things
I can't dissect
For all these things
that I regret
For all these things
I smoke and drink
For all these things
that make me think
For all these things
the young and the old
For all these things
Do what you're told.

*For all these things
I can't get past
For all these things
I want to last
For all these things
One day they'll be clear
For all these things
No more fear.*

I'm falling apart
but, no one can tell
The feelings I feel
I really can't show
The things I've done
mostly things you can't see
among all of these things
somewhere is me

Where are you?
Are you looking for me?
Do you feel as lost as I do?
Do you wonder if anybody out there thinks like you?
Will you recognize me, or will I be too late,
or will you?
Please don't give up. I am here.
You are okay. You're not alone, not anymore.
The feeling you felt but couldn't feel, is real.
And it's here and it's now.
It won't ever go away, it won't falter.
It will only grow with us.
We'll jump into this life together knowing we'll do everything
that until now was only in our dreams.
We'll accept each other's thoughts, agree to disagree.
We'll go across the country and discover it and its people, each other and ourselves.
Knowing instantly when we see it.
When will all this be real?

*bright as the sun
constance of the tides
forever changing like the clouds
of a summer sunrise
the enchantment of the moon
knowledge like the stars
rooted to the earth
touched with mystic powers
Where in this world?
When in this life?
When will it end,
this continual strife*

*I know what my future holds
Though it's out of my control
Coming from the middle
the center of my soul
It's the reason I am here
And why I've little fear
In the things I'm meant to do
If you look real close, it's clear
Something I can't hide behind
It seeps from my insides
All part of some crazy plan
Is where my future lies*

viscous cycle
so engrained
forever imprinted
on our brain
going so unnoticed
somehow wanting change
but god has it planned
just so, arranged

*Lost inside
these open walls
changing lives
like a dress-up doll
trying to find
something to stand on
much more fun
is reckless abandon*

New name, new place
new life, new face
fresh start, head smart
this is starting over

*For all the things I gave
you were not full of me
you had to break my trust
and briefly sanity
But I will be okay
better men have tried
to break my heart completely
But, still I am alive
It isn't always easy
to keep my hope alive
It gets me through the day
Sometimes it's all I have*

*Without a reason
or a name
standing here
in cold and rain
it soaks the bones
chills the heart
searching dark skies
clouds hide the stars*

*Just past tomorrow
but before yesterday
glistens the future
fading the pain
free falling through time
destiny solid ground
sliding to a future
lost and then again found*

Why would you say,
if it isn't true?
Why present yourself,
if it isn't you?
Why tell lies,
that only cause pain?
Why come to me,
only to leave again?
Why do I care,
when it can only hurt?
When did life,
become so perverse?
How can it feel so natural,
to want what isn't right?
What does it mean,
when to you love is a fight?
When yelling is a whisper.
When tears do feel like rain.
When night just brings another tomorrow
and happiness is back then.
A time you can't remember,
that feels just like a dream
and life becomes this place,
you just can't seem to leave.

For as hard as it is right now
at least it's not like before
no worries of coming home
I know now, I can do more
to go all the places
freely dream all the dreams
find pictures in the clouds
life in the streams
and the most important
I've found in the end
the promise to myself
I'll never do it again

To be but a star
What a view of the world
Watch it spin out of control
How small we must seem
Forgotten detail in a dream
Lost among our goals

*Thank you for the memories
They'll never leave my mind
and for the night before the last
for letting me enjoy
for keeping clear the vision
and the ability to see through
all the miscellaneous
the beautiful, true you*

Watching the earth
renewing itself
appreciating the new
the joy of rebirth
following the butterfly
as it hovers above
taking in nature
a vision of love
all that was gone
seems to return
another year passed
What did you learn?

The softness of feathers
warmth of a summer sun
depth of the ocean
it's only just begun
to flow through the veins
a fresh spring leaf
it will not last forever
the beauty is in the belief
eternity's too long
to plan for what's to come
enjoy today's mystery
all there is to count on

Fairies dance, they twirl
they surround me
hovering above the grass
I am lost in them
so light the breeze carries them
so true they shine with light
Oh, to fly among the flowers
feel the nectar on your toes
hide behind the grasshopper
watch him chatter with the gnomes

*Divorce done quickly!?!
It's taken me years
to build up this strength*

Closing the door
unlocking my eyes
say good-bye to old friends
and even older lives
let go of the past
in one final stand
turn and walk away
say good-bye to this land
move on to the future
uncertain for sure
can't stay here forever
you're meant for much more

I don't want
to take anymore
I don't want to
read or learn
crawl in the corner
and squirm
let go of all these lies
the mindless peoples
advice
the uncertainty in your
eyes
no more follow through
no more fading blues
I give up
my life to you
to do with it what you choose
So fuck it if I lose

Colors merge in beauty
adding contrast to our life
changing what was thought to be
what was true and what was right
giving sunshine the chance to show
exactly what one can do
changing life as colors dance
lost in loving you

*For I who thought
that never would
have been proved
wrong once again
and passing days
as well they should
have healed in many ways*

Once and again, I've learned to let go
Opened my heart, have taken a chance that could explode
Thinking of things only the ocean should know
Watching the earth as it dies just to grow
Following a breeze to the sun as it lows
Do you see the people; they'll just stand there in rows
Not sure of saying yes, not willing to say no

*The tiniest grain of sand
Is what makes the pearl
Just like the words that
Decide the little girl
Where shall lie the future?
What shall I become?
What is it that balances
Responsibility and fun?*

*Thank you for waking me
And for making me cry
Thanks for the lesson learned
That lets me die inside
And for the harsh words
But, don't forget the guilt
Why don't I want you?
Because it makes me hurt*

Lucky for me
The big picture I see
Your insecurity
The thing that won't let you sleep
Or let me be free
Your doubt seeps in, unfortunately

*Why is it that a small bump in the road can cause so much distress?
Is it the bump, the road, or how we handle the both of them or how we handle each other, or ourselves?
It would be so much easier to just move past it.
Rather than focus on it, where it came from, how it got there, what it wants, what it means.
We'll be here all day analyzing <u>this</u> bump.
While we miss a million others.*

Ocean, land
Sun, sand
A beautiful place to be
Wind and love
The clouds above
A union of you and me

*Though I may not live like this
I will surely live
Debt and gold will come and go
I will continue to give
Beyond my means, beyond my dreams
Life to the extreme*

*My stubbornness is my determination
And independence creates inner strength
Curiousness is a virtue
Restraint through practiced patience*

If I give you all my mystery
Where shall the secrets lie
If it were to all come so easily
Why would we bother to try
Without a questing mind
Or a curious eye
The interest that intertwines
Could so sadly become a sigh

*If only but one season stayed
And last throughout the year
How unfortunate a change delay
No chance to reappear*

Fall leaves shuffle on the street
Like small crustacean at the beach
Though cool air now keeps them buried deep
The chill of winter becoming clear
As the colors dance from clouds to ground
Before the hibernation, beauty abounds

My lips beg to smile
taken by your beauty
impressed by your mind
humbled by your endurance
and the love in your eyes

*Women are resilient
and it shows in the way
they always continue onward
day after day after day*

*Sense matters little
To a fortune teller bride
Stand in the corner
Or run and hide
Wide open spaces
To yell and to scream
You can't shut me out
For I am the queen*

Follow the stars
Watch where you fly
Open your eyes
Take in the sky
Get swallowed into life
Learn to let go
Let your dreams be your guide
You know what you know.

At ocean side
On sunny day
Waves shall dance
While seashells wash away
Dunes will back my daydream
As pipers line the shore
The army of my future
I, I stand before

Greenery lines the ocean
Turning to the sun
Planted in ancient beauty
Where the seasons never done
Every shade of color
The sun on the horizon
I turn to watch the ocean
And the tide as it comes in

And what of all these breezes?
And what does lie below?
What about tomorrow,
Next where shall I go?

beauty is in nature
it shines in the dew
it emanates from the flowers
and at last, reflects in you
rising in the morning
disappears at dusk
allowing the stars to light the sky
a guiding light to trust
for every changing season
has a time to come
and everything that must
will find a way to be done

*Breezes blow your cares away
The tide washes you clean
Able to leave all worries behind
Now feel free to dream
You can't do this just anywhere
It takes a special place
And I can't explain how good it feels
To drop out of this race
To find my place along the side
And watch these people run
To where they don't know
Just hurry and get done*

*the road that we travel
with turns and yields
flowers and trees
grass and fields
the emotions we feel
love and pain
time keeps going
sun and rain
look out for the laughter
it softens the blow
of the wind outside
the cold, the snow*

Reflecting upon a day
Spattered with idle time
Watching green pastures
Drinking red wine
Time well spent
In the eyes of my mind
Time wisely wasted
In beautiful sunshine

Floating along a distant shore
My thoughts cry out to you
The wings beat strong and carry on
A feeling of renew
A breeze brings them in
Emotions soak the skin
The beauty of what one can do

Praise and blame
It's all the same
Other people's opinion
To raise you up
Then cut you down
Some unseen king's dominion

Upon opening the door
Envision bright colors galore
And there she stood so plain
As soon as her eye met mine
The tears snuck up from behind
Some beautiful memories bring pain
She spoke a gentle voice
Emotions left no choice
I wondered what she had seen
For her years were many
My mind went empty
Humbled by her soul so serene

Falling from the sky
Passing through a cloud
Feeling the adrenaline rush
It all does come around
Now is the time
For a bird's eye view
And I'll be learning to fly
All my energy refueled
Tomorrow is as far away
As yesterday is past
Take a chance, live today
Memories are what last

*What an awful place
We wake and sleep
The nature of this beast
Where everything dies
And is then reborn
Only to do it again
What purpose does lie in belief?*

To what do we owe displeasure?
Our sorrow is our fate
To never truly be rid of all
The memories engrained
To whom do we owe displeasure?
Impossibly denied
The ups and downs of life itself
But, a roller coaster ride
So why try to hide
From what you can't even find
Accept life for what it is
Pleasure and pain forever intertwined
Such is a life like this

Oh, how I try
To plant this seed
Yet it unearths itself
But I dig deep
On my self it feeds
A time I just can't keep
With water and sun
A life all its own
It just wants to blow away
A journey just begun
Wings need to be flown
If only for a day
To stand by and watch
Keep one eye on the clock
Choices come too late
One more notch
The doors unlocked
Nothing to make you stay

A beautiful bouquet of flowers
Fresh cut, in a wild mix
Of colors and sizes
Petals and leaves
Each one has a special niche
Cared for daily
But still they fade
Time goes by
Days will change
Their beauty cannot stay

Passing through
In this life
Once I met a boy
Although he left
And came again
We did not say good bye
I wonder where
He is right now
And if he's thinking of me
For moments pass
And time does fly
As life can only be

Aloof as a cloud
Rolling down a mountain
Happiness as children are
Splashing about a fountain
Scattered as the squirrel
That plays among the trees
Free as the birds
That float along the breeze

*Octobers surely here
You feel it in the air
Smell it on the breeze
Watch it rustle the leaves
Enjoy the crispness of outside
And take in all you can
For all too soon the seasons change
It ends as it began*

A change has begun
If in only an hour
Forever's unspun
Bloomed as a flower
This thing opens doors
To worlds never seen
With such familiarity
Like the memory of a dream
Where shall it lead?
A path never ending
To forever and back
And again to the beginning

*Beauty lies in unturned rocks
And on a rainy day
Hidden in thoughts,
And old grandfather clocks
Sometimes in the things we don't say
Every change of the season
From beginning to end
It's all for a reason
The beauty is in the meaning
And always found in friends*

On this day and every other
A thought has come to me
And like the one whom I longed to dis-
cover
I wandered desperately
Until I found a way of my own
Where finally I was free
To seek and find
Relax and unwind
And found true destiny

*She is the one
with angel's wings
who touches down
for a taste of spring
she herself
is in everything
this the one
with angel's wings*

does spring exist at all
under cold and snow
only the brown leafy remnants
are what does lie below
as the wind gives up its chill
the sun becomes more clear
and death gives way to life
mother nature's eternal right

fate will guide you
if only you listen
to be sent out
on your own special mission
to follow the dreams
with the most personal meaning
have faith in the future
you have to keep going

*To spend all your life
living someone else's dream
what a waste of potential
of the time in between
Now
and the day
an uncertain future
holds the joy of possibility
and a sense of adventure*

*Talking with the trees
as they argue with my thoughts
their opinion can't be bought
or persuaded with any ease
stuck with an honesty
that comes from years of growth
the roots of the great oak
the palm and its pliancy*

she soars like an angel
above the blue sky
so satisfied with life
never questioning why
she never takes a chance
cannot take a risk
such is the life of an angel
real life is what is missed

A miracle grows suddenly
with a subtle longing for more
is it greed that makes us search
for the bigger picture
Is the truth in the details
or hidden by them

I see beautiful trees
that have withstood the fastest winds
during the coldest times.
Growing small and strong.
Living and growing through years of changes
Never saying a word about what is being done to their world

*Softness surrounds me
as your words invade
the truth flows
just beneath the surface
befuddled words
fall from my grasp
while I try to keep composure
do you notice?*

*Oh spirits find me
let me follow the butterfly
to the truest of answers
let me sleep on the ground
as to absorb your wisdom
be warmed by your sun
to heal my cold heart
and keep faith in what is to come*

Blank page
fill with thought
let this pen
pierce my brain
to let the words
pour out
let them run
and soak the pages
then dry
with crusty truth

must be obedient
for the call cannot be ignored
outside a stranger waits
no use in denying fate
the mind inquires, and words slip
leaving ideas to linger
where does the line of reality lie?
Where do hands fall
When eyes close?
the lids a private screening
for the future left unknown
envision all that could be
real or imagination
what should be, will come
to truth from the illusion

a secret beauty
lies,
waiting to be found
in a moment or a whisper
it could become real
yet,
fear
keeps it silent
shyness
keeps it secret
time
keeps it still
while wonder
helps it grow

a knock in the dark
stirs my sleep
I wander down the hall
wondering of the visitors intention
I touch my hand to the knob
and turn slowly
there you stand
two steps from the bottom
soaked from raindrops
breathing heavily with impatience
holding firm in your own presence
here on my step
in the darkness of night
must we speak now
and drown in the labels
that fall from our mouths
they could only be a distraction
let us keep silence
as our only restraint
and indulgence
as our discipline
no longer need to question intention
it's blazing from behind your eyes

*I dreamed I was once
a small purple flower
on Assateague Island
I grew and bloomed and died
and then
on to something else
but for one brief moment
I was a small purple flower
and I bloomed*

You are only as trapped
as you let yourself be
follow through
leads to breaking free

flip through the pages
who falls out
which come to mind,
become mine
these pages are time

shaves of ice fall from the sky
a wondrous, beautiful nigh`
ponds with their crystal cover
a pile of sticks hide the otter

our eyes are meeting
and it is subtly said
our ice is melting
times quickly spent
I'm drawn to you
though our words are plain
the innermost truths flow
below the surface again
How long must I hold my tongue
I wish to be enlightened at once

*small wondrous creature
with the amazing power of flight
your chest heaves
as if it may burst
I desire your freedom*

*Is it strange that I have
so few questions
such little fear
so sure it will work
one day at a time
the future is ours
and you, for now
all mine*

Meir Sprite
to the world's delight
was born both
soft and strong
his life, well lived
has much to give
to each of us and beyond
the blink of his eyes
ignites fireflies
with the energy
from earth and above
a sly smile of his mouth
brings joy to this house
and will fill his space with love

We walked the mountains
and studied the beach
enjoyed the trees, the sea
and now....
the sun is your smile
the clouds your eyes
You live in the sunset
I greet you when the sun rises
although you no longer
share my days
you have now
become my days

You, me and the moon

This is where we'll be
that's what we'll do
You, me and the moon

We'll talk it through
and maybe cry some too
You, me and the moon

You love me
and I love you
You, me and the moon

across all time
what ever we may do
You, me and the moon

Close your eyes
tomorrow will be new
You, me and the moon

A List of First Lines

A beautiful bouquet of flowers 141

A change has begun 149

A knock in the dark 181

A miracle grows suddenly 167

A secret beauty 179

Aloof as a cloud 145

And so she kept running 27

At ocean side 115

Beauty is in nature 119

Beauty lies in unturned rocks 151

Blank page 175

Breezes blow your cares away 121

bright as the sun 45

climbing up the mountain 33

Closing the door 77

Colors merge in beauty 81

Divorce done quickly 75

Does spring exist at all 157

Fairies dance, they twirl 73

Fall leaves shuffle on the street 105

Falling from the sky 133

Falling through the sky 23

Fate will guide you 159

Flip through the pages 187

Floating along a distant shore 127

Follow the stars 113

For all the things I gave 55

For all these things 37

For as hard as it is right now 63

For I who thought 83

Greenery lines the ocean 117

I don't want 79

I dreamed I was once 183

I know what my future holds 47

I look upon the world 29

I see beautiful trees 169

I see you as a glowing beam of light 15

I see you in my darkest hour 25

I'm falling apart 41

I'm trapped in this place 13

If I give you all my mystery 101

If only but one season stayed 103

Is it strange that I have 195

Isn't it strange, the way people flow 9

Just past tomorrow 59

Life is what we see 19

Lost inside 51

Lucky for me 91

Meir sprite 197

Must be obedient 177

My lips beg to smile 107

My stubbornness is my determination 99

New name, new place 53

Ocean, land 95

Octobers surely here 147

Oh How I try 139

Oh spirits find me 173

On this day and every other 153

Once and again 85

Our eyes are meeting 191
Passing through 143
Praise and Blame 129
Reflecting upon a day 125
Sense matters little 111
Shaves of ice 189
She is the one 155
She soars like an angel 165
Small wondrous creature 193
So full of life 31
Softness surrounds me 171
Spinning in circles 35
Talking with the trees 163
Thank you for the memories 67
Thank you for waking me 89
The road that we travel 123
The softness of feathers 71
The things in this life 21
The things that we do 7
The tiniest grain of sand 87

Though I may not live like this 97

To be but a star 65

To spend all your life 161

To what do we owe displeasure 137

Upon opening the door 131

viscous cycle 49

Watching the earth 169

We pass through time 11

We walked the mountains 199

What an awful place 135

Where are you? 43

Why is it that a small bump in the road can cause so much distress? 93

Why would you say 61

with dirty hands 17

Without a reason 57

Women are resilient 109

You are only as trapped 185

You, me and the moon 201

www.ingramcontent.com/pod-product-compliance
Lightning Source LLC
Chambersburg PA
CBHW071217090426
42736CB00014B/2855